Will God Forgive Me,

Can I Be Saved?

A SCRIPTURAL EXAMINATION
OF THE UNPARDONABLE SIN AND THE
SAVING POWER OF JESUS CHRIST

Jon Hunter

Author of "Saving Michael, A Bulimia Story"

ISBN 978-1-0980-8413-4 (paperback)
ISBN 978-1-0980-9070-8 (hardcover)
ISBN 978-1-0980-8414-1 (digital)

Christian Faith Publishing, Inc.
832 Park Avenue
Meadville, PA 16335
www.christianfaithpublishing.com

All scripture quotations are taken from the KJV.

Printed in the United States of America

Introduction

— ⌘ —

Nicodemus, a ruler of the Jews, came to Jesus by night and confessed, *"Rabbi, we know that thou art a teacher come from God: for no man can do these miracles that thou doest, except God be with him."* Jesus knew what Nicodemus needed to hear, telling him *"Except a man be born again, he cannot see the kingdom of God."* (John 3:2–3)

This declaration that Jesus made to Nicodemus is a revelation to all who seek forgiveness and eternal life. If we want to see heaven, then we also must be born again. Many fear they cannot be forgiven for one particular sin or a multitude and are afraid they are unable to experience this new birth, which is God's gift of salvation.

The following is to share God's way of forgiveness. No matter what you've done, no matter what sin or sins you've committed, you *can* be forgiven. You *can* have a personal relationship with Jesus Christ, and you *can* receive His gift of eternal life. God's Word is clear about this important truth. Whosoever desires forgiveness and salvation can be saved, and *whosoever* means you.

The Blasphemy of the Holy Spirit
The Unpardonable Sin

D rawing from my personal inquiry of Christian pastors, there seems to be an endless concern experienced by some individuals—those who fear they have committed a sin, or sins, that cannot be forgiven. These sins range from lying, theft, abortion, adultery, rape, murder, and beyond. Many people are filled with overwhelming feelings of guilt, and they do not know how to find assurance of forgiveness and reconciliation to God.

In Matthew 12:31, Jesus tells us that *all* sins are forgivable, except one. "*Wherefore I say unto you, All manner of sin and blasphemy shall be forgiven unto men: but the blasphemy against the Holy Ghost shall not be forgiven unto men.*"

We are going to examine the one and *only* sin that cannot be forgiven. Looking at the evidence given us by God, we will determine what this sin is, who might be guilty of this sin, how one can *know* whether they are guilty, and why this sin is *not* forgivable.

The following is a personal testimony about my search for salvation through Jesus Christ and the spiritual battle that ensued. Just as there is a God who loves us and desires to save us from our sins, there is also a regiment of demons, determined followers of Satan, who, with great fervor, are committed to keep us from ever coming to know Christ. It seems that the intensity of spiritual attacks vary greatly between individual believers, but these attacks are somewhat common and very real.

As we survey the following challenging scriptures, some of which bring fear to many who misunderstand their true meaning, it is important to recognize that *whosoever* desires salvation and pardon from God *can be saved*. If you are afraid that you are lost without any hope of forgiveness, "*lift up your heads; for your redemption draweth nigh*" (Luke 21:28b).

My Search for God,
God's Search for Me

———— ✐ ————

There is nothing more important in a person's life than to have a personal relationship with Jesus Christ. The decision one makes about trusting in Jesus will make the difference between spending eternity in heaven with God or being forever separated from Him. All too often, people are *not* prepared for the most important event in their life, which is death.

When I was a young adult, I too was not prepared to face the Lord. I went to church each Sunday, prayed occasionally, and I believed in God—that is, I believed that God existed. This is a common phrase I've heard from other people, the I-believe-in-God confession. But what does believing in God really mean, and does believing that God exists secure one's eternal destiny? James 2:19 tells us, *"the devils also believe, and tremble."*

Regrettably, fearfully, even though I believed in the existence of God the Father and Jesus His Son, if I would have died, I would have been eternally lost. I would have then been delivered to eternal judgment.

Most of the world is in the same condition I was in. Everything seems all right between you and God, and when you die. You soon find out that everything was *not* all right, but at that point, it's too late. When you take your final breath and step into eternity, there are no second chances. A person must prepare for the next life *before* they get there.

I did grow up in a Christian home, at least, with a Christian mother. My father considered himself to be a Christian, but until late in his life, he didn't bear any evidence that would attest to that. It was shortly before his death that he truly trusted in Christ and was saved.

My mother took me to church every Sunday while I was growing up. We attended a church just outside of Columbus, Ohio. Our pastor, who I will refer to as Reverend Harold, was a kindhearted man who led our congregation. I suppose that he was the epitome of what I thought a good pastor should be. Each Sunday, he would preach one of the messages that our denomination's diocese would distribute to its congregations across the country.

It would be a feel-good message, talking about God's love for us and the need for us to love one another, while including an inspirational story about life. The one missing ingredient in our worship services was the Gospel, sharing with those in attendance what was essential to have a real relationship with Jesus Christ.

During that time, I felt that everything was fine between God and me. When I sinned, I would ask for forgiveness and believed that He would forgive me; it was as simple as that. I also held to the beloved Bible verse in John 3:16: "*For God so loved the world, that he gave his only begotten Son, that whosoever believeth in him should not perish, but have everlasting life.*"

Not understanding what this precious Bible verse was actually saying, I thought that if I believed that Jesus existed and that He was the Son of God, it meant that I was a Christian. I didn't understand that John 3:16 speaks of having a personal relationship with Christ and putting my faith in His sacrificial death on the cross to pay the penalty for my sins.

When I was sixteen years old, I met and fell in love with my first and only girlfriend, Sherry, who also became my wife of over forty-six years. Sherry came from a non-Christian family but did have a mother that allowed her and her siblings to attend church.

When we started dating, Sherry began going to church with me. I soon found out that she had never been baptized. Even though I had no real knowledge of biblical doctrine, I felt that baptism was something that Sherry needed to experience. Reverend Harold agreed to baptize Sherry but insisted that she go through a short counseling session to help her understand what the purpose of baptism was.

I attended this session with Sherry, along with another couple from our church. Since this occurred nearly fifty years ago, I don't recall exactly what was said during this informative event. I do remember though what occurred at the end. Reverend Harold prayed a prayer of salvation with us, telling each of us to repeat the prescribed words after him. We all asked Jesus to forgive us of our sins and to be our Savior.

I had been witnessed to before but had no real understanding of the Gospel of Christ. After praying, the reverend asked each of us individually whether we believed that we were saved. Sherry, along with the other two attendees, responded yes; they did believe that they were saved. When Reverend Harold asked me, I told him no; I didn't think anything happened when I prayed. I was spiritually blind to the entire process of salvation.

After my surprising response, Reverend Harold firmly told me, "Yes, you *were* saved." He meant well, but he was wrong. I wasn't saved when I prayed because I didn't understand what being born again was all about.

During the class, I asked Reverend Harold about one particular portion of Scripture that I had run across during my very limited Bible reading: "*Therefore I say unto you, all manner of sin and blasphemy shall be forgiven unto men, but the blasphemy against the Holy Ghost shall not be forgiven unto men*" (Matthew 12:31).

I was concerned that apparently there was one sin that could be committed by a person which could not be forgiven by God. I asked the reverend about this, wondering how someone might know if they, possibly unwittingly, had committed this horrible sin and were doomed to eternal punishment. The reverend *correctly* assured me that if a person is fearful that they might have committed this sin, their concern is proof that they had not. I accepted his response, but I still had an uneasy feeling about the possibility of unintentionally committing this sin at some point in my life.

Sherry and I were married in 1974 and continued attending Sunday services at my church, under the leadership of Reverend

Harold. We were invited to teach a Sunday school class to four-, five-, and six-year-old children. The sad fact was I was not a real Christian. I was not a born-again believer, and I should not have been teaching children about the Savior that I did not have a personal relationship with.

I believe that during this time, the Lord was actively seeking me. I had the opportunity to read two wonderful Christian books. One was *The Cross and the Switch Blade* written by Pastor David Wilkerson, which was an excellent book for young adults seeking God. Another book was *Joni* written by Joni Eareckson Tada. Joni's life story spoke to me in a very meaningful way. I began to truly desire a relationship with the Lord. My dilemma was, according to Reverend Harold *and* my mother, my spiritual life was fine and my relationship with God was complete.

It wasn't until I was twenty years old that my mind and heart were opened, and I finally understood the Gospel. I was taking evening classes at a small technical school in Downtown Columbus at the time. I was driving home one evening, pondering the things of God, when suddenly I understood. It was as if a dark cloud had been lifted from my mind, and I knew that Jesus died to take the punishment for our sins. He did this so that he could, in exchange for our unrighteousness, give us His righteousness and the gift of eternal life. I also believed in my heart that if I would have been the only person to accept Him as Savior, Jesus would have given His life just for me.

Even though I finally had a grasp of God's process of salvation, I didn't realize that I needed to ask for or accept it. I am confident, though, that when a person truly believes the Gospel and decides in their heart to put their trust in Jesus for their salvation, salvation has, at that moment of true faith, already taken place; and a prayer of acceptance is confirmation of the presence of saving faith and the beginning of a new spiritual life. Although I did not fully understand it at that moment, by God's grace, I became a Christian. From that point on, my life began to change, and I started to earnestly seek the Lord.

My Fifteen Years of Desperation

As a new Christian, I had so much to learn. I remember one day, a Sunday school student asked me if Jesus is God. "No," I responded. "Jesus is the *Son* of God." I had never been told that Jesus was the Almighty. Again, I had no business teaching Sunday school. It was time though that the Lord was going to send me through a life-changing period of chastening and learning. I believe the reason for this was that God wanted me to seek and follow Him with all my heart.

One of the obstacles I was facing was the church we were attending because the services were lacking in scriptural instruction. Sunday after Sunday, they were filled with social messages, not solid Bible teaching, which is of critical importance for spiritual sustenance and growth. I was now starving for God's Word.

Not long after becoming aware of salvation by grace, I was lying awake in bed in the middle of the night. I was again thinking about the verse in Matthew concerning the unforgivable sin, the sin of blasphemy against the Holy Spirit, when suddenly a wicked thought came into my mind. It was an evil thought concerning the Holy Spirit. I don't know why this thought came about, other than possibly because my fear of committing this sin was so intense that the fear itself created a self-fulfilling prophecy and pushed this thought into my mind.

I was terrified. This was a thought that I did not want, but it had still come upon me. Its intensity and clarity was horrifying. I didn't know what to do. I recalled what Reverend Harold had told me, how my concern about committing the unpardonable sin was proof that I had not, but I was not convinced. I lay awake in bed praying, begging for God's mercy. I tried to go back to sleep and waited for the morning.

I went to work the following day feeling a bit more at ease, but I knew that I needed to talk to somebody to find an answer of peace. I called Reverend Harold and went to meet with him in his office that afternoon. When we sat down, I explained to him what had happened. I was hoping for some enlightenment from the Scriptures, something biblically solid that I could hold onto for assurance.

The reverend reminded me that we had already discussed the subject of the unpardonable sin and what he had said about my fear being proof that everything was all right. He told me a little story that "we cannot keep a bird from landing on our head, but we can keep it from building a nest in our hair," suggesting that we can't control all of our thoughts but we can keep those thoughts from dominating our mind. This was similar to the feel-good messages that our church was good for, but it offered me no real peace or answers to my problem.

The reverend gave me a little packet of cards containing popular Bible verses and told me to memorize a different verse each day. He seemed unable though to show me scripture which could provide assurance that I was all right spiritually.

I did have the one Bible verse that helped me feel more confident that I had not committed the sin spoken of by Christ. John 3:16 told me that if I believed in Jesus, I was saved. So I determined that if I believed in Him, I could not have committed the unforgivable sin. That, combined with my fear, gave me a small level of hope that everything was all right between the Lord and me.

As time passed, I tried to feel more secure about my relationship with God. I want to point out that feelings have *nothing* to do with salvation. I felt close to the Lord before I was really born again. It was after I was saved that all my insecurities developed.

Many people feel that their relationship with God is fine, possibly because of the feel-good messages that are preached each week from numerous pulpits around the world. These messages spew forth from pastors who fail to share the truth about the need for Christ and His salvation. How sorrowful so many people will be when they finally meet Jesus face to face at judgment, and He tells them, "*I never knew you: depart from me*" (Matthew 7:23).

The day came when Reverend Harold left our church, suddenly accepting a position at a church in California, so our congregation was left without a pastor. During this time, I tried to become more involved in other areas of worship, including attending a new but very shallow Bible study that was being offered at our church. By now, I had learned more about the Bible during self-study than I ever did during our worship services. I think the most frightening aspect of that is so many churches are, like our church was, offering no real scriptural substance to lead people to Christ.

When the Darkness Came

———— ✑ ————

It seems that, often, spiritual attacks come upon a believer in the middle of the night. I had developed a limited amount of peace about my relationship with God since my fearful experience with the unpardonable sin had occurred. My mind though had still been troubled for some time, almost as if this fear was trying to drive itself into my life again in a covert way, possibly coming from an outside spiritual force.

As I was sleeping one night, I had a fearsome dream. In my dream, I was standing in a region of darkness. Off in the distance, out of the black, I could hear the voice of someone crying out, "IS THIS HELL?" and then I heard the sound of horrible screaming. Somehow, I knew that the person who was spiritually lost and screaming in the distance was me. This nightmare had a horrible effect on my confidence regarding my relationship with God. I still held on to John 3:16, trusting that as long as I believed that Jesus was the Son of God, I was saved.

I was now about to enter a new level of spiritual darkness that would take me close to the point of suicide, but these trials would eventually open my eyes to truths of the Bible that God wanted me to understand.

Sherry and I decided to take our Sunday school class on a trip to the Columbus Zoo. As we sat in our car, waiting to pick up one of our students for the trip, I suddenly experienced an overwhelming sense of darkness engulf my mind, truly my entire being. I cannot describe the experience, other than it was some form of evil spiritual oppression and it had to do with my fears of being eternally lost and my faith in Christ.

I began suffering from a deluge of unwanted blasphemous thoughts—thoughts attacking the Lord and the Bible, thoughts that were trying to draw my mind into doubting the very existence of God. This cloud of darkness was attempting to draw me away from my faith. I believe that it was some type of demonic attack. I was filled with a sense of foreboding, and it would not go away.

The mainstay for my hope of salvation was my having faith that Jesus was the Son of God. That was the rock that gave me confidence that I had not committed *the* sin, the unforgivable one. My error was that I was depending on the strength of *my* belief, *my* level of faith on one point of doctrine, rather than solely trusting in the one person who could save me "*to the uttermost*," Jesus Christ (Hebrews 7:25). When a person depends on anyone or anything less, especially one's own self, they will fall short and may be lost. It is ultimately the faithfulness of Christ that saves us. The faith that we have in Jesus is a gift from Him and is a result of the saving grace of God.

I tried to rid myself of this demonic cloud hanging over my mind but was unable to do so. I was flooded with doubts about Jesus, believing that if I could not bolster my faith in Christ again, there was no hope for my salvation.

I began searching the Scriptures, looking for reasons to believe, but every time I found a verse that would give credibility to the Gospel and the Lordship of Jesus Christ, that verse would be countered by evil thoughts and doubts. The devil is very skilled in the art of twisting the truths of the Bible. I have found though that the Scriptures are the one true offensive weapon God has given us that evil cannot stand against. Ephesians 6:17b shares that we are to take up "*the sword of the Spirit, which is the word of God,*" not only to defend our faith but to defeat our spiritual enemies.

By that time, it had become nearly impossible for me to read the Bible. When I did, I was barraged by those horrible thoughts. I became fearful to open the Bible's cover because of the blasphemies that would overwhelm my mind. I had fallen into a deep dark pit of confusion, and I did not know a way out.

"Bet your soul" was my next pestering thought. Any time I would question something, the thought would come: "Bet your soul," or "Sell your soul to the devil." This occurred thousands and thousands of times. I would then have the need to follow those thoughts with a quick prayer, asking the Lord to "please release me from the bondage of that thought!" This would cycle through my mind many times each day, going through this over and over again until my brain was numb. This struggle went on for many years.

I thought that by now I had surely committed the unpardonable sin because of these wicked thoughts that were overwhelming me, and now I did not have confidence that I really believed Jesus was the Son of God. What I didn't understand at the time was my battling against this unseen force, which was attacking my faith, was evidence that I really did believe in Christ. My inner faith was the driving force that caused me to cling to Him in the midst of this satanic assault.

When the powers of darkness come to attack the minds and hearts of those who belong to Jesus, no matter how hopeless things seem, we must not lose hope. The Almighty God is still in control, watching over and caring for us. The Apostle Paul writes in Romans 8:31, *"If God be for us, who can be against us?"*

The very devils of hell may come to assault us, and in our own strength, we would be defenseless. But nothing can separate us from the powerful hands of Almighty God.

My Search for an Answer

———— ⟳ ————

B ecause our church no longer had a pastor, each Sunday, someone from the congregation would volunteer to speak; but there was no one to sit down and personally counsel with about spiritual problems or concerns.

Not long before our pastor left, our church hired an older gentleman from the congregation to work in the church office. He would answer the phone and do some of the clerical duties associated with the church's operation. I knew that I needed to talk with someone, *anyone*, about my fears; so I decided to take my growing pile of reference material and speak with this man. I was sure that, being a mature Christian, he would be willing to give me some insight in how to deal with my confusion and shore up my fears about being lost.

I went to the church office unannounced but felt certain that this man would be kind and understanding about my plight. I sat down and explained my problem to him; and with all his Christian love and compassion, he responded, "Well, first of all, I want you to understand that I don't care, when you leave here, whether you feel any better about your problem or not." To make sure I understood what he was saying, he repeated himself, saying the same thing over again. Apparently, he didn't feel it was his duty to show compassion to another person, maybe because it wasn't listed as part of his job responsibilities. He did listen to my story and shared his few thoughts with me in a shallow way, finally finishing by handing me a stack of paperwork to assist him with his duties since I held him up from his work while sharing my problem with him.

He insisted that I go on visitation with him and one other person to meet with several people who had come to our church. We had an opportunity to talk with a woman who had visited the previous Sunday. She expressed concern about not wanting to go to a church that preaches salvation by grace alone. She just felt that "becoming a Christian couldn't be that simple." This gentleman assured her that she wouldn't hear any of that at our church, which was probably true. As I said, I had never knowingly heard the Gospel preached from our pulpit by anyone.

I continued searching the Scriptures, looking for hope of my salvation. Using a study Bible that I had purchased, I frequently cross-referenced verses, seeking a more comprehensive understanding of what each Bible verse was actually meaning and what was happening in my spiritual life. I started reading the book of Hebrews, where I came across two additional scriptures that brought new terror to my soul.

> For it is impossible for those who were once enlightened, and have tasted of the heavenly gift, and were made partakers of the Holy Ghost, And have tasted the good word of God, and the powers of the world to come, If they shall fall away, to renew them again unto repentance; seeing they crucify to themselves the Son of God afresh, and put him to an open shame. (Hebrews 6:4–6)

I was confident that I was saved the night I understood and believed the Gospel, but because of my blasphemous thoughts and doubts about Christ, I was fearful I had fallen away from the faith.

Also, Hebrews 10:26–31 brought me even greater horror:

> For if we sin willfully after that we have received the knowledge of the truth, there remaineth no more sacrifice for sins, but a certain fearful looking for of judgment and fiery indignation, which shall devour the adversaries. He that

despised Moses' law died without mercy under two or three witnesses: Of how much sorer punishment, suppose ye, shall he be thought worthy, who hath trodden under foot the Son of God, and hath counted the blood of the covenant, wherewith he was sanctified, an unholy thing, and hath done despite unto the Spirit of grace? For we know him that hath said, Vengeance belongeth unto me, I will recompense, saith the Lord. And again, The Lord shall judge his people. It is a fearful thing to fall into the hands of the living God.

Needless to say, because these verses seemed so threatening, I was sure they were meant for me. I was especially fearful about chapter 10, verse 26, "*For if we sin wilfully.*" I had sinned knowingly many times during my life, times that I would eventually ask for forgiveness afterward. Because of my ignorance about the true meaning of these verses, I was sure that I could not be forgiven and was unable to be reconciled to God.

My spiritual and emotional life had fallen apart. I was on the verge of becoming psychotic. I spent many hours on my knees, praying, begging God, and crying out for His mercy and forgiveness. How I wished that I had not been born or that I was an animal that wouldn't have to face the judgment of God after death. I believe that I would have committed suicide to escape this terror, but I was scared I would then be sent to the very judgment that I feared. To make things even worse, I heard a radio pastor share his belief that God doesn't hear the prayers of the lost other than the prayer of salvation. I had prayed and prayed for God's mercy, but now I was scared that the Lord wasn't hearing my prayers anymore because my relationship with Him wasn't right.

I can remember wishing that God was like Jesus, who was so merciful, still not understanding that Jesus is God. I could see in the New Testament the love and compassion of Christ. If God were as merciful as Jesus, perhaps He would have pity on me and forgive me. I was drowning in a sea of confusion, which is precisely what the powers of darkness wants for each of us. The more I tried to secure a foundation for my faith in Jesus, the more my faith was assaulted.

New Hope

———— ∽ ————

One evening, I was contacted by a man in our church. Harvey, one of our church officers, was seeking assistance in moving some furniture for an elderly woman from her home to a retirement apartment. I was glad to help because I was hoping to talk to somebody, *anybody* that might have even a little insight into what I could do to escape the judgment that I knew was looming in my future.

Harvey was a good man to talk to. After sharing my problem with him, he told me that he believed that I *was* saved, but he would contact a retired pastor friend to find out if he would take time to speak with me. This former pastor said to come over to his home and he would see if he could help.

The man listened to me carefully as I shared the horrors I was facing. He told me that he didn't believe that I had rejected Christ. He explained to me that the unpardonable sin is the act of refusing God's gift of salvation, deliberately with open eyes and doing that *permanently*. If a person did commit this sin, the Holy Spirit would withdraw His conviction, and there would no longer be any remorse in the person's life concerning the loss of a relationship with God.

I accepted his explanation but only to an extent. I didn't understand how his description of this sin corresponded with the scriptures in Matthew, Mark, Luke, or Hebrews. I also was still having severe problems with wicked thoughts and attacks on my faith in Christ. I was scared that the assault on my faith was a sign that I *had* permanently rejected Jesus and I couldn't regain faith again to repent and be saved.

I heard about a book on Christian apologetics, *Evidence that Demands a Verdict* written by Josh McDowell. This newfound resource did help to shore up some of the doubts that I was having, but the powers of darkness knew my areas of weakness and worked all the more to confuse me. Each portion of scripture which provided evidence to support the Lordship of Jesus Christ would quickly be countered by a demonic accusation to dispute that scriptural evidence.

During this time, God yet again showed His kindness to me. Sherry and I had gone camping with my sister and her husband. I was hesitant to share my problems with family, but I finally talked with Margo about my spiritual struggles. She told me about a book titled *Grace Abounding to the Chief of Sinners* written by John Bunyan, who also authored the well-known classic *Pilgrims Progress*. John Bunyan's book was an autobiography of his Christian life and the extreme spiritual assaults he faced as a young believer. In many ways, John's problems were similar to my own, including fear of committing the unpardonable sin and warring against evil thoughts. His book was a long-needed breath of fresh air for my life and gave me renewed hope for my relationship with God.

I had an opportunity to talk with a knowledgeable pastor in a large Bible-believing church in Columbus. I spoke with him about my problem with unwanted blasphemous thoughts which seemed to permeate my mind when I read the Bible or thought about the things of God. He told me that he had counseled others with the same problem and that he believed it was a form of demonic attack. He also said that there was no scriptural evidence that demons can read our minds but they can contaminate our thinking.

The Lord allowed me to meet Pastor Bob Burney, former pastor of Calvary Bible Baptist Church in Westerville, Ohio, and now a Christian radio talk show host, author, public speaker, and close friend. My brother had recommended that I speak with Pastor Burney and possibly visit his church, which Sherry and I did during a Wednesday night service and again the following Sunday. Pastor Bob led a congregation of Bible-believing, Christ-loving individuals.

His ministry was to introduce people to the Lord Jesus and teach and preach the Word of God.

What a wonderful experience it was to be taught from God's Word. The messages flooded my soul with faith and hope in Jesus. Sherry and I immediately became members of this congregation of Christ-loving people. We soon developed friendships with virtually everyone in the church, some of which are still active friendships today, over forty years later.

I continued struggling with my fears and doubts. I talked to my new pastor about my problems but still didn't find a solid scriptural solution.

Pastor Bob, along with the other believers I talked to, tried to assure me that when I accepted Christ, I was saved. No matter what was in my past, God had forgiven me. I often worried though that when people tried to calm my fears, they suspected that possibly I had no hope but were trying to console me by hiding the truth. I finally concluded that God didn't want me to seek a solution from men. He wanted me to depend on Him and His Word alone for answers to my concerns.

My fears and confusion continued with varying intensity for over fifteen years. I felt hopeless so many times, yet each time that it seemed there was no hope, God gave me something to hold on to, just enough to keep me from completely giving up.

Facing My Fears

———— ✑ ————

My dilemma was that I didn't understand how men's explanation of what the unpardonable sin was fit into the scriptural context of the Bible verses in Matthew, Mark, Luke, and Hebrews.

I determined that I was going to have to study each scripture and verse, word for word, to try to understand what the Lord was saying. I found that I needed to read not only each of the terrifying Bible verses but also the adjacent verses to fully comprehend what these scriptures meant.

My first goal was to prove to myself that I had not committed the unpardonable sin. I discovered that the terms *unpardonable sin* and *unforgiveable sin* are not found in the Bible. These are labels that men have given to these scary portions of Scripture, but they don't necessarily reflect what God was wanting to communicate to the reader.

After a *thorough* examination of the frightening verses in the book of Matthew, I realized that these scriptures did contain stern warnings from God to motivate us to seek and cling to Christ, but they were not speaking of an accidental sin committed unwittingly by a person or even words of a blasphemous nature spoken carelessly by an individual. These verses speak of the *deliberate* act of turning away from and *forever* rejecting Jesus, and this warning was given *specifically* to the Pharisees who were falsely accusing Christ of casting out demons by Satan's power rather than that of the Holy Spirit.

Wherefore I say unto you, All manner of sin
and blasphemy shall be forgiven unto men: but

24

the blasphemy against the Holy Ghost shall not
be forgiven unto men.

And whosoever speaketh a word against the
Son of man, it shall be forgiven him: but whosoever speaketh against the Holy Ghost, it shall not
be forgiven him, neither in this world, neither in
the world to come. (Matthew 12:31–32)

One common mistake people make is to read verses in the Bible
without studying the full context of the scripture. The first word spoken by Jesus in Matthew 12:31 is *wherefore*, tying verse 31 in with the
previous verse. If we read Matthew 12:30, Jesus tells us:

He that is not with me is against me; and
he that gathereth not with me scattereth abroad.

This scripture warns that when a person does not gather with
Christ, they will tend to go astray, wandering away from Him and
the Gospel, eventually scattering abroad—just like a lamb which is
inclined to stray from a shepherd, determined to go its own way.
Such a person desires to purposefully be loosed from any ties of being
ruled by Christ.

The rulers of Israel were living in a time of expectation of the
imminent arrival of the Messiah. Prophecies concerning the coming
of Christ actually pointed to the time in history that Jesus was here in
the flesh. The Pharisees also understood that the countless miracles
done by Jesus verified His claims of Lordship. He restored sight to
the blind and hearing to the deaf; Jesus calmed the raging storm. He
fed thousands of people with just a few loaves of bread and small fish.
He even raised the dead. No power under heaven, other than that of
Almighty God, could perform miracles such as those that Jesus did.
Nicodemus attested to this in the book of John 3:1–2:

There was a man of the Pharisees, named
Nicodemus, a ruler of the Jews: The same came
to Jesus by night, and said unto him, Rabbi, we

know that thou art a teacher come from God: for no man can do these miracles that thou doest, except God be with him.

This scripture tells us that the Pharisees recognized Jesus's miracles as evidence that He was sent by God. This also reveals that not all the rulers in Israel were against Christ. Many of the Pharisees though had become quite prideful and self-serving in their hearts. They loved the glory and honor they received from men because of their status, so they would not accept or openly confess Jesus as the Messiah.

Jesus knew their pride and hardness of their hearts. Possibly the clearest example of the Pharisees' deliberate rejection of Jesus is revealed in the parable in Mark 12:1–8:

And he began to speak unto them by parables. A certain man planted a vineyard, and set an hedge about it, and digged a place for the winefat, and built a tower, and let it out to husbandmen, and went into a far country. And at the season he sent to the husbandmen a servant, that he might receive from the husbandmen of the fruit of the vineyard. And they caught him, and beat him, and sent him away empty. And again he sent unto them another servant; and at him they cast stones, and wounded him in the head, and sent him away shamefully handled. And again he sent another; and him they killed, and many others; beating some, and killing some. Having yet therefore one son, his wellbeloved, he sent him also last unto them, saying, "They will reverence my son." But those husbandmen said among themselves, "This is the heir; come, let us kill him, and the inheritance shall be ours." And they took him, and killed him, and cast him out of the vineyard.

In this parable, the landowner represents God the Father. The husbandmen represent the corrupt scribes and Pharisees, the rulers of the Jews. The servants represent the prophets, and the beloved son is Jesus. The parable shows that the husbandmen clearly recognized who the servants sent to the vineyard were and that these servants carried with them power granted by the landowner; but the husbandmen treated them cruelly, disregarding their authority, beating some, and killing others. When the landowner finally sent his beloved son, the husbandmen also recognized who he was, knowing he was the heir; and they believed that killing him would assure them possession of the fruits of the vineyard.

The parable reveals that the husbandmen recognized the identity of the heir when they took him captive and killed him. Even so, the rulers of Israel recognized that the evidence supporting Jesus Christ as being Lord and Messiah verified His claims; but they still rejected, arrested, and crucified Him.

This is where we begin to understand the gravity of the Pharisees' false accusation concerning this miracle of Christ. By claiming that Jesus was casting out demons by any power other than that of the Holy Spirit was ludicrous. As Jesus said in Matthew 12:26, "*And if Satan cast out Satan, he is divided against himself; how shall then his kingdom stand?*" It is also interesting that the Pharisees only made this accusation concerning Christ's miracle of casting out demons and not about His many other miracles which were clearly God ordained. Though the powers of darkness do have some *limited* control or power over nature, which is seemingly miraculous (*see Exodus 7:11–12 and Job 1:13–19*), miracles of such great magnitude which were accomplished by Christ (*e.g., calming the sea, feeding the five thousand, and restoring life to those long dead*) involve supernatural power which emanates from Almighty God alone (*Exodus 4:11 and 8:16–19*).

These religious leaders had but one goal, and that was to create doubt in the eyes of the people of Israel regarding the Lordship of Jesus Christ. They were not only running in the opposite direction of repentance and faith in Jesus, but they were also attempting to lure the people of Israel away from following Him.

Whether these leaders had actually crossed a line of no return is not clear. But being in the position these men were in, seeing Christ's miracles and His righteousness, and knowing the prophesies concerning the Messiah, they still not only rejected Him but *fled* from faith in Him and attempted to draw the people of Israel away from Him. This shows that repentance was quite unlikely. What more would motivate the rulers of Israel to repent and believe, knowing what they already knew and seeing what they had already seen? That is why their false accusations against Christ were so damning. Their allegations revealed the *extreme* hardness of their hearts. It was then most likely impossible for them to repent. Thus, there would be no forgiveness for this horrible sin.

It's important to understand that whosoever comes to Jesus for mercy *will* be accepted and forgiven by Him, though the heart of a man can eventually become so hardened that they will never come to Christ for forgiveness. This is because they may never again have the desire to do so.

After reading this additional scripture in Matthew, I began to understand the purpose of Jesus's warning. When the Holy Spirit reveals the truth of the Gospel to an individual, it's a dangerous thing to deliberately delay accepting God's gracious offer of salvation, lest one becomes hardened to the truth and the invitation from God then has no effect. (As Matthew 12:30 explains, if a person is not heading toward and clinging to Jesus, he is pushing Him away and straying from Him.) He might then reach a point where it is impossible to turn back to seek Christ again and will, in the end, die lost.

Jesus said, *"And whosoever speaketh a word against the Son of man, it shall be forgiven him: but whosoever speaketh against the Holy Ghost, it shall not be forgiven him, neither in this world, neither in the world to come."* Speaking against the Son of man implies speaking against Christ in His veiled form of manhood. Speaking against the Holy Ghost is the act of *deliberately* speaking in opposition to the Holy Spirit's revelation and glorification of Jesus. It is the Spirit of God that opens a person's heart to believe in Christ. Blaspheming or speaking against the Spirit involves a *deliberate* and *continuous* hardening of a person's heart to resist what the Spirit is saying, and that hardness reveals itself through the person's words and lack of repentance.

When the rulers suggested that the miracles of the Holy Spirit were satanically empowered, while knowing that the visible and scriptural evidence proved otherwise, indicated a tremendous wickedness and disrespect for God's power and holiness. This ultimate and ongoing rejection of the truth forever prevented repentance.

Jesus gave this warning to the religious rulers of Israel because they of all people should have recognized Jesus as their Messiah and His miracles as being accomplished through God's power. If at any time these wicked men would have repented and turned to Christ, He would have accepted and forgiven them; but for those sorrowful individuals, because of the hardness of their hearts, repentance was most likely impossible.

The Frightening Verses
in Hebrews

Years ago, I had a brother-in-law who, for the sake of anonymity, I will refer to as Jim. Jim claimed to be a born-again Christian. In fact, he went to a Presbyterian seminary to become a pastor. After graduating, the elders of his church did not feel that Jim had an appropriate personality to lead a church. This rejection that my brother-in-law experienced was so devastating emotionally that he left the Christian faith. Jim eventually converted to Judaism, ultimately denying the Lord Jesus. He finally divorced my sister because she would not follow him in his conversion. Jim has never returned to faith in Christ.

> For it is impossible for those who were once enlightened, and have tasted of the heavenly gift, and were made partakers of the Holy Ghost, and have tasted the good word of God, and the powers of the world to come, if they shall fall away, to renew them again unto repentance; seeing they crucify to themselves the Son of God afresh, and put him to an open shame. (Hebrews 6:4–6)

Falling away is a source of concern for many believers. A born-again Christian is eternally secure, meaning that the powerful hand of God will not allow a true believer to stray to a point of no return.

A good shepherd would never knowingly allow one of his lambs to wander off into danger unattended.

When my sister's husband left Christianity, even though he appeared to be a believer, he apparently had never owned saving faith. Jim had intellectual knowledge concerning the things of Christ, but he didn't have the Holy Spirit dwelling in his heart. He never fully surrendered his will or his life to Jesus, so bitterness overpowered his artificial faith.

The Bible in 2 Timothy 3:5 speaks of someone *"having a form of godliness, but denying the power thereof."* Jim did exhibit a *form* of godliness. He knew Gospel terminology and was involved in Christian circles. Jim was also highly educated but, unfortunately, educated in *liberal* theology. He always appeared to have doubts about the accuracy of the Bible. It seemed that Jim took great pride in his level of education, but when he was rejected by the church elders, he was driven by such bitterness that he eventually turned against Christ. This could not have happened if Jim were truly born again. In 1 John 2:19, the apostle confirms this. Speaking of apostates in the New Testament church, *"they went out from us, but they were not of us; for if they had been of us, they would no doubt have continued with us: but they went out, that they might be made manifest that they were not all of us."*

Sometimes when a shepherd of biblical times had a lamb that would insist on straying, he would break one of the lamb's legs. The shepherd would then mend the broken leg and carry the lamb on his shoulders. He would hand feed and lovingly care for the lamb until the leg was healed. From that time forward, the lamb would not stray again. Though this practice seemed harsh, it would save the lamb's life because it would keep the lamb safely under the shepherd's protective care and away from the dangers it would have faced when away from his watchful eye. In the same way, God will not allow His children to permanently stray from the faith and will work without ceasing to keep us securely and fully dependent on Him.

There are some who look at this doctrine of eternal security with question and doubt because they view it as a possible license to sin, worrying that if a believer feels secure in their salvation, he or she might take liberty and fulfill the desires of the flesh. This is due to a failure to understand that redemption is truly a gift from God and that mankind can add nothing to their salvation. It is God who gives us the desire and ability to live a sanctified life. A true believer will not chase after a life of sin. Though often tempted and sometimes falling prey to the desires of the flesh, a child of God will ultimately hold true to his faith in Christ.

When we consider the shepherd and the wandering lamb, when the lamb's leg was broken, it would have been quite painful and incapacitating. The broken leg made the lamb helpless and fully dependent on the shepherd.

Even so, the Lord knows how to lovingly chasten those who are truly His children, sometimes in painful ways; but He does so to keep us repentant and dependent on Him. God's chastening is not a punishment for sin; Jesus suffered the punishment for our sins on the cross. Chastening though *is* for our correction and learning. A born-again believer cannot lose his or her salvation by sinning but can suffer painful consequences from the hand of our Heavenly Father. We are secure in our salvation but not because of our works or self-righteousness. It is the gracious sacrificial gift of Jesus at Calvary and His faithfulness that saves us, and it is His watchful eye that keeps us from falling away.

In Hebrews 6:4–6, Paul writes that there were some in the church who were "*once enlightened*," who had "*tasted*" of the heavenly gift, the good Word of God, and the powers to come. They had even been partakers of the Holy Ghost but were never actually saved.

When the apostle speaks of those who were once enlightened, he is speaking of those who had an intellectual knowledge of Jesus and the Gospel, just like my brother-in-law Jim who appeared to have faith. He knew all the Christian terminology, enough to claim Jesus as Savior, but he eventually turned away from Christ. Even though Jim appeared to be a Christian, if he had been a true believer, he could not have completely left the faith.

The word *tasted* suggests that the person has only taken a small sample of something without committing to share in a full meal. Some in the early church appeared to have trusted Christ. They may have even been baptized and participated in fellowship with other believers, but when persecution arose, they eventually left the faith. They were "*partakers of the Holy Ghost*" but in an incomplete manner. The Holy Spirit may have dwelt with them but not in them. They saw, and perhaps even benefited, from miracles done by the Spirit but had not personally received Him permanently in their hearts, not to the point of salvation. This is demonstrated in Jesus's parable about spreading the seed of the Gospel.

> And some fell on stony ground, where it had not much earth; and immediately it sprang up, because it had no depth of earth: But when the sun was up, it was scorched; and because it had no root, it withered away. (Mark 4:5–6)

Jesus interprets this parable in Mark 4:16–17:

> And these are they likewise which are sown on stony ground; who, when they have heard the word, immediately receive it with gladness; And have no root in themselves, and so endure but for a time: afterward, when affliction or persecution ariseth for the word's sake, immediately they are offended.

In these verses, Jesus speaks of those who at first accept the Gospel with joy, but afterward, when trials or persecution comes, they leave the faith. This occurs because there is no real faith or "root" to provide the needed sustenance to sustain them spiritually.

> Seeing they crucify to themselves the Son of God afresh, and put him to an open shame.

After leaving Christianity, these apostates at times openly turned against Jesus, crucifying Him anew in their hearts and putting Him to an open shame by blaspheming His name.

This is the falling away that Paul is talking about, not just a temporal slipping back into sin and then repenting but the total, deliberate, and permanent turning against Jesus. Such a falling away from Christ so hardens the human heart that it is, in the end, impossible to repent. Impossible because nothing will ever draw that person back to trust in Jesus. After coming so close to having real faith, they turn back to their old condition of unbelief. What more could occur to make them believe? Just as the rulers in Matthew 12:31 who witnessed Jesus miracles but refused to accept Him as their Messiah, nothing more could be done to bring them to trust in Him.

How can someone have assurance that they will be accepted by Jesus again after slipping into sin? The desire in a person's heart to repent and turn again to Christ is proof that the opportunity for repentance still exists because that desire comes from the Holy Spirit. If a point of no return had been reached, there would be no desire in that person's heart to return to Christ. As the apostle tells us in Hebrews 6:6, "*It is impossible to renew them again unto repentance.*"

Will God Forgive My Willful Sins?

ᴄℐℴ

While cross-referencing Bible verses, I discovered Hebrews 10:25–31:

> Not forsaking the assembling of ourselves together, as the manner of some is; but exhorting one another: and so much the more, as ye see the day approaching. For if we sin willfully after that we have received the knowledge of the truth, there remaineth no more sacrifice for sins, But a certain fearful looking for of judgment and fiery indignation, which shall devour the adversaries. He that despised Moses' law died without mercy under two or three witnesses: Of how much sorer punishment, suppose ye, shall he be thought worthy, who hath trodden under foot the Son of God, and hath counted the blood of the covenant, wherewith he was sanctified, an unholy thing, and hath done despite unto the Spirit of grace? For we know him that hath said, Vengeance belongeth unto me, I will recompense, saith the Lord. And again, The Lord shall judge his people. It is a fearful thing to fall into the hands of the living God.

When studying the Bible, it's important to understand what context the scripture you're reading is set in, examining not only the adjacent text but also recognizing to whom it was written. The writer of this letter to the Hebrews was speaking primarily to Jewish believers. These early Christians were encouraged to hold fast to their new-found faith in Christ. Temptation was coming from outside forces, attempting to lure these young believers to return to the Jewish church. It takes the divine gift of saving faith from God for a person to remain faithful to the Gospel in the midst of such an assault.

These spiritually young Christians were instructed to mature from being milk fed and to grow into accepting the meat of scripture concerning Christ. The writer tells us in Hebrews 10:25: "*Not forsaking the assembling of ourselves together, as the manner of some is; but exhorting one another: and so much the more, as ye see the day approaching.*"

Persecution was not coming only from the Jews but also from Rome. The Lord would sometimes use such persecution to expose those who were not truly saved. Believers need to examine their own lives to make sure that they are steadfast in the faith. When a person faces spiritual trials which attack what they believe, they may either be lured away from the faith, revealing their actual condition of unbelief, or have their faith strengthened, confirming their position in Christ.

The "*sin wilfully*" in verse 26 has been the source of fear for many people. At first glance, it would appear this would include any sin committed with the full knowledge of the sinner. God understands us and the weakness of our flesh. The reason we need a Savior is because we are sinners. In our unsaved condition, we are helpless to overcome sin. It is the indwelling of God's Spirit through the new birth that empowers us and gives us victory over fleshy temptations.

In the following text, Paul describes a believer's battle with the sinful desires of the flesh:

> For we know that the law is spiritual: but
> I am carnal, sold under sin. For that which I do
> I allow not: for what I would, that do I not; but

what I hate, that do I. If then I do that which I would not, I consent unto the law that it is good. Now then it is no more I that do it, but sin that dwelleth in me. For I know that in me (that is, in my flesh,) dwelleth no good thing: for to will is present with me; but how to perform that which is good I find not. For the good that I would I do not: but the evil which I would not, that I do. Now if I do that I would not, it is no more I that do it, but sin that dwelleth in me. I find then a law, that, when I would do good, evil is present with me. For I delight in the law of God after the inward man: But I see another law in my members, warring against the law of my mind, and bringing me into captivity to the law of sin which is in my members. O wretched man that I am! who shall deliver me from the body of this death? I thank God through Jesus Christ our Lord. So then with the mind I myself serve the law of God; but with the flesh the law of sin. (Romans 7:14–25)

When we are saved, our old nature dies; in fact, Paul says that our old corrupt nature was crucified with Christ on the cross.

I am crucified with Christ: nevertheless I live; yet not I, but Christ liveth in me: and the life which I now live in the flesh I live by the faith of the Son of God, who loved me, and gave himself for me. (Galatians 2:20)

At the moment of salvation, we are given a new nature, the perfect sinless nature of Christ. The Holy Spirit comes and dwells inside our heart, and over time, changes in our life will become apparent. Paul writes in verse 18: *"For I know that in me (that is, in my flesh,) dwelleth no good thing."* Our dependence on the Holy Spirit for victory over temptation is essential. If we try to serve and obey God in the strength of our flesh, we are destined to fail. Jesus tells us in John 6:63: *"It is the spirit that quickeneth; the flesh profiteth nothing: the words that I speak unto you, they are spirit, and they are life."* The new birth is a spiritual experience. Our flesh is still sinful, carrying with it all manner of ungodly desires.

Paul tells us that there is a constant battle between the flesh and the spirit and this will likely continue until we go to be with the Lord. Through chastening, the Lord weakens our flesh and its desires, better enabling us to overcome temptation; but the battle between flesh and spirit in this life never completely ends. As believers, we all suffer from the problem of willful sin to one degree or another, and it is a problem we need to address. Otherwise the chastening hand of God may come upon us—not a vengeful hand of the Father but a loving hand of correction and mercy. Those who are not chastened by God do not truly belong to Him.

> But if ye be without chastisement, whereof all are partakers, then are ye bastards, and not sons. (Hebrews 12:8)

When the writer speaks of this willful sin, he tells us, *"there remaineth no more sacrifice for sins, But a certain fearful looking for of judgment and fiery indignation, which shall devour the adversaries."* The willful sin he is speaking of is the one of permanently turning away from Jesus, the same falling away spoken of in Hebrews 6:4–6. This is a turning against Christ, the one whom this apostate had supposedly trusted for salvation but afterward rejected, returning again to the religion of the Jews, never again returning to Christ. This sin cannot be committed by someone who is truly born again but can be committed by a person that had *seemingly* trusted Christ and who, after coming so close to salvation, permanently turns away from the Savior.

The writer is saying that Jesus was now the only sacrifice for sin that is acceptable to God. There remained no other sacrifice that could cleanse a person from their iniquities. If a person turned against Christ to the extent of permanently rejecting Him, what else could be offered to God as recompense for transgressions? Paul isn't speaking about someone who has just temporally slipped back into sin. A true Christian might fall into grievous sin but later come to repentance.

In the Old Testament, there were those that despised the law of Moses. Despising the law speaks of someone who had rejected the law and the authority that God gave Moses to the point of open rebellion. For those who did so, the sentence was death. How much more should the punishment be for someone *"who hath trodden under foot the Son of God* [treading upon the Savior like a common doormat, the only begotten Son of God who came to suffer and die for our sins], *and hath counted the blood of the covenant, wherewith he was sanctified, an unholy thing* [someone who has considered the precious blood of the Savior which was shed to provide forgiveness for our sins as though it were common and unholy], *and hath done despite unto the Spirit of grace* [committing the sin spoken of in Matthew 12:31–32 by hardening one's heart against the Spirit's revelation of Christ to the point of never repenting, never turning again to Jesus for forgiveness]." For the person who is guilty of this transgression, there remains only one end, and that is the final judgment of God. *"For we know him that hath said, Vengeance belongeth unto me, I will recompense, saith the Lord. And again, The Lord shall judge his people. It is a fearful thing to fall into the hands of the living God."*

How can a person know if they have committed this horrible sin, and can a person have assurance that they can still be forgiven? By the promise of the Lord Jesus, *whosoever* desires forgiveness and salvation *can be saved.* We know this because a person who has permanently turned against Christ will never again desire to turn back to Him. The desire that someone possesses to turn again to the Savior is evidence that the Holy Spirit is calling him to repentance.

Might It Be Too Late to Repent?

The final scripture that hindered my peace with God was Hebrews 12:16–17:

> Lest there be any fornicator, or profane person, as Esau, who for one morsel of meat sold his birthright. For ye know how that afterward, when he would have inherited the blessing, he was rejected: for he found no place of repentance, though he sought it carefully with tears.

Esau was the eldest son of Isaac and twin brother of Jacob. Though Jacob and Esau were brothers, they could not have been more different in their personalities and spiritual standing before God. The Lord had great plans for Jacob, choosing him to be the father of the nation of Israel. Esau would father the nation of the Edomites.

According to Genesis 25:28, Esau was loved by his father Isaac because he ate of Esau's venison. Esau was Isaac's firstborn, which was a position of special blessing and was considered a place of honor by God.

Genesis 25:29–34 tells us:

> And Jacob sod pottage: and Esau came from the field, and he was faint: And Esau said to Jacob, Feed me, I pray thee, with that same red pottage; for I am faint: therefore was his name

called Edom. And Jacob said, Sell me this day thy birthright. And Esau said, Behold, I am at the point to die: and what profit shall this birthright do to me? And Jacob said, Swear to me this day; and he sware unto him: and he sold his birthright unto Jacob. Then Jacob gave Esau bread and pottage of lentiles; and he did eat and drink, and rose up, and went his way: thus Esau despised his birthright.

Esau had returned from a day of hunting, apparently having no success finding game, when he happened upon Jacob preparing some of his red pottage. As Esau eyed the food that had been prepared by Jacob, it must have looked so appealing, and he knew that it would be a good meal, one that he desperately desired.

Esau asked Jacob for some of his red pottage. Jacob was a cunning man who wanted something that his elder brother possessed. He told Esau, "*Sell me this day thy birthright.*" Now the birthright was something that should have been considered very precious by Esau. The firstborn received not only a special blessing from his father but also a double portion of the inheritance. The firstborn would also be head of the family when the father died, eventually ruling over his younger siblings.

Esau said to Jacob "*I am at the point to die: and what profit shall this birthright do to me?*" Esau wasn't really at the point of death, but his lust for immediate gratification of this fleshy desire caused him to make a very poor decision by selling his birthright and swearing it to his younger brother.

Men often make poor, even spiritually fatal decisions, to follow the desires of the flesh rather than Christ.

The bowl of red pottage was probably very satisfying to Esau for a moment, and he doubtlessly left his brother Jacob feeling full and satisfied. But in the end, the cost of the meal was everything. When it came time for Esau to receive his father's blessing, it was too late. His blessing had been given to his brother Jacob, to whom Esau willingly sold it for a morsel of food. When Esau sold his birthright to Jacob, he failed to consider the ultimate cost of such a poor decision.

> For ye know how that afterward, when he
> would have inherited the blessing, he was rejected:
> for he found no place of repentance, though he
> sought it carefully with tears. (Hebrews 12:17)

Many who live carelessly in this life, when facing God's final judgment *after* death, will desire to repent, begging for Christ's mercy; but it will be too late. Eternal decisions will have been made. Just as Esau sought to repent, he could not regain his birthright or the firstborn's blessing "*though he sought it carefully with tears.*"

Those who choose the pleasantries of this life rather than fellowship with God and those who seek eternal salvation through anything other than the sacrificial blood of Jesus will cry out in protest when they face Christ at His judgment seat. Jesus said in Matthew 7:22–23:

> Many will say to me in that day, Lord, Lord,
> have we not prophesied in thy name? and in thy
> name have we cast out devils? And in thy name done
> many wonderful works? And then will I profess
> unto them, I never knew you: depart from me,
> ye that work iniquity.

Myriads of souls who were and are deeply religious. Many who profess Christ and even do great works in His name will fail to secure salvation by His grace, trusting instead in the good works that they have done. Attempting to be good enough to enter into His kingdom by their own righteousness, they will stand before Jesus, never having put their faith in His precious blood that was shed for the sins of mankind. Many will do this because they will not have heard or understood the Gospel, perhaps because they worshiped in a church that failed to preach the truth. The church leaders may have filled their services with feel-good messages rather than preaching about God's gift of salvation. It was by God's grace that I came to know Jesus personally. The trials that I experienced during my early years of seeking Christ took me on a search that eventually led me to salvation. Even though the fears I faced were terrifying, they made me aware of my need for a Savior, and seeking answers to my fears ultimately gave me a solid basis for faith. I learned what and why to believe.

The Lord reveals the truth of the Gospel "*to them who are the called according to his purpose*" (Romans 8:28). He clearly makes known the reality of salvation by grace through His Word so those who are being misled, along with the leaders of their congregations, are without excuse. Sadly, their lack of understanding may lead to their eternal loss.

The Way of Salvation
What It Means to Believe in Christ

―――――― ❦ ――――――

The overwhelming theme of the New Testament is that we need to believe in Jesus to be saved. But what does it actually mean to believe in Jesus? This believing is not just an acknowledgement of Christ's existence. It is the act of trusting or dependence on Jesus, making a deliberate and conscious decision to place one's faith in Christ's righteousness and death on the cross for our salvation.

One of the concerns I had during my times of trial was whether or not I had saving faith. There is an intellectual level of knowledge that a person can possess regarding Jesus: believing He existed, that He was a good person or teacher, perhaps accepting that He is the Son of God, but still not be a Christian.

Before I was truly born again, I assumed I had a relationship with Christ, but I didn't. Countless lost souls go to church each week, never knowing about or hearing the Gospel. Many pastors refuse to see the need for a Savior. The shed blood of Jesus doesn't fit in with their social gospel. Those that attend these dead churches may believe that their relationship with Christ is fine, but sadly, they may actually be lost.

In the third chapter of book of John, the apostle tells us:

> There was a man of the Pharisees, named
> Nicodemus, a ruler of the Jews: The same came
> to Jesus by night, and said unto him, Rabbi, we
> know that thou art a teacher come from God: for

no man can do these miracles that thou doest,
except God be with him.

Nicodemus was a religious ruler of the Jews, one though who
seemingly had not succumbed to the lust for glory that many of the
other Pharisees possessed. He approached Jesus by night, probably
fearing retribution from the other less virtuous rulers. Nicodemus
confessed to Jesus that they (the Pharisees) knew that He had been
sent by God because of the mighty miracles that Jesus had done.

Jesus understood what Nicodemus needed to hear before he
asked. *"Jesus answered and said unto him, 'Verily, verily, I say unto thee,
Except a man be born again, he cannot see the kingdom of God.'"* Even
though Nicodemus was a religious teacher, a ruler in the nation of
Israel, he did not understand how to, with certainty, secure eternal
life.

Jesus responded to Nicodemus's greeting without hesitation.
He told this teacher of Israel that if he were to ever see the kingdom
of God, he *must* be born again. *"Nicodemus saith unto him, 'How
can a man be born when he is old? Can he enter the second time into
his mother's womb, and be born?'"* Nicodemus was struggling with
the problem of confusing spiritual issues with the physical, asking
Jesus whether a man must reenter his mother's womb and be born a
second time.

> Jesus answered, "Verily, verily, I say unto
> thee, Except a man be born of water and of the
> Spirit, he cannot enter into the kingdom of God.
> That which is born of the flesh is flesh; and that
> which is born of the Spirit is spirit. Marvel not
> that I said unto thee, Ye must be born again."

If *we* truly desire to see the kingdom of God, then we also must
be born again. The Apostle John wrote, *"For God so loved the world,
that he gave his only begotten Son, that whosoever believeth in him
should not perish, but have everlasting life"* (John 3:16). But how do

we believe in Jesus to be saved? The Apostle Paul writes in Romans 10:9–10:

> That if thou shalt confess with thy mouth the Lord Jesus, and shalt believe in thine heart that God hath raised him from the dead, thou shalt be saved. For with the heart man believeth unto righteousness; and with the mouth confession is made unto salvation.

And in verses 13–14:

> For whosoever shall call upon the name of the Lord shall be saved. How then shall they call on him in whom they have not believed? and how shall they believe in him of whom they have not heard?

Paul tells us that if we confess with our mouth the Lord Jesus and believe in our heart that God raised Jesus from the dead, we *will* be saved. The confession that Paul is speaking of is most likely the confession which is made during baptism. This profession of faith is not the way a person acquires salvation; but it is the revealer, or evidence, of the inner saving faith which has been given to the believer as a gift from God, bringing them to the act of confession. Paul says that we first need to *hear* the Gospel before we can believe. When the gift of faith then becomes evident in us—that is, in our heart—we have the ability to earnestly call upon the name of Jesus for salvation.

> For by grace are ye saved through faith;
> and that not of yourselves: it is the gift of God.
> (Ephesians 2:8)

With our heart, we believe unto righteousness, meaning that we secure our relationship with Christ by faith, that faith which is provided to us *without* works. This faith is freely given to us by the Holy

Spirit. Baptismal confession is then important because it is ordained by God as a public acknowledgment of that gift of faith. If a person does not have true faith in Christ, baptism is meaningless. Baptism is not the way we receive salvation. Baptism is the ordained way we publicly confess our faith in Christ.

"How then shall they call on him in whom they have not believed?" Many years ago, my wife and I shared the Gospel with my wife's sister Tammy. She seemed happy to hear about Jesus and prayed a prayer of salvation. She went to church with us that morning and, with much coaxing, went forward during the invitation to make her decision public. Afterward, we saw no change in her life. There was no evidence of real faith or repentance. I suspect that her prayer of salvation was motivated by the desire to save face with my wife and me rather than having a sincere longing to belong to Christ. Many years later, we found out that Tammy was dying from cancer. We again shared the Gospel with her, but her heart had become so hardened that she could not understand or accept what we were saying. When she prayed for salvation many years earlier, she didn't have true faith in or a real desire for a relationship with Christ, so her prayer for salvation was meaningless.

At the end of each service at the Billy Graham crusades, Pastor Graham provided an opportunity for those who desired to accept Jesus to come to the front of the stage and receive salvation. It was always very moving to see the amazing response to the invitation given by Pastor Graham. Though multitudes would respond, occasionally, a few people went forward with wrong motives, possibly because friends did and they didn't want to stand out as being different. When they prayed a prayer for salvation, asking Jesus to be their Savior, if they did not truly understand their need for Jesus or did not really desire to accept Him as Lord of their life, their prayer was of no effect. They lacked conviction, or genuine faith, to understand their desperate need for Jesus and to receive His gift of salvation.

Paul does assure us that *"whosoever"* shall call upon the name of the Lord, doing so for salvation and having a real desire to be forgiven and accepted by Christ, will be saved. The concern that I faced during my time of trial was how could I know if I had authentic faith, or enough faith, to be saved? The Scripture makes this clear: *"How then shall they call on him in whom they have not believed?"* Unless a person has an ulterior motive for calling upon Jesus, their prayer for salvation is evidence that they have real faith, *saving* faith; and so they will be saved. We are not saved because of our level of faith. We are saved because of our decision to turn away from our old life of sin and rebellion to have an authentic forgiven relationship with Jesus Christ.

Jesus tells us, *"No man can come to me, except the Father which hath sent me draw him"* (John 6:44). Your desire to come to Christ comes from God's invitation through the Holy Spirit. We can have assurance of God's acceptance because He first called us to come to Him. Without His first calling us, we would never, with real desire, call upon Him for salvation.

This calling upon Christ, spoken of by Paul, is calling upon Him, not just for anything but specifically for salvation. Many people call upon Jesus in prayer every day without understanding their need for Him as Savior. In my youth, I prayed to Jesus for anything and everything, but I did not recognize my need for redemption. Entire religions have been brought to life which include Jesus in some way but fail to accept the need for His sacrificial death for man's sin.

We do have the assurance from God's Word that no matter what is in a person's past, no matter what sins you have committed, whosoever with a sincere heart and desire calls upon the name of Jesus for salvation *will* be saved.

Two Men and the Savior

I believe that the clearest example of someone accepting Christ in the New Testament is revealed in the account of the two men who were crucified with Jesus. Matthew and Mark refer to these men as thieves. John calls them malefactors, and Isaiah writes that they were both wicked individuals. Whatever their crimes, they both were basically alike, two hopeless souls seemingly cut from the same mold. They almost certainly had lived godless lives and were now facing certain death and, afterward, God's judgment.

During the crucifixion of Jesus, the crowd who passed by His cross cried out scornfully saying, "*He trusted in God; let him deliver him now, if he will have him: for he said, I am the Son of God. The thieves also, which were crucified with him, cast the same in his teeth*" (Matthew 27:43–44).

This crowd of observers, some who took pleasure in watching the suffering of others, would stay close to Golgotha, the place of Roman brutality and execution. Jesus, now crucified, hung on His cross in agony while onlookers mocked, crying out that He trusted in God, let God save Him.

As Jesus suffered this cruel mockery, one of the two thieves who was being crucified with Him experienced a change of heart. Seemingly, God, by His grace, opened this man's eyes to understand the truth; and so he came to believe in Jesus.

When the other *impenitent* thief cried out, "*If thou be Christ, save thyself and us,*" this penitent man rebuked him saying, "*Dost not thou fear God, seeing thou art in the same condemnation? And we indeed justly; for we receive the due reward of our deeds: but this man hath done nothing amiss. And he said unto Jesus, Lord, remember me when thou comest into thy kingdom"* (Luke 23:39–42).

Jesus, so close to death, had suffered more cruelty at the hands of sinful man than any other person could. Now, at the pinnacle of Jesus's anguish, this thief who had certainly lived a life of wickedness cried out to Him for mercy. There was no longer time for this lost man to become a better person or start going to worship at the temple, no opportunity to try to work his way into God's kingdom. A man who is crucified could not be more helpless. The only thing that he could offer Jesus were his sins and a prayer for mercy.

Jesus, out of His loving compassion, responded to this man, *"Verily I say unto thee, Today shalt thou be with me in paradise"* (Luke 23:42),

Because he cried out to the Lord, he was accepted by Him without hesitation and was given the gift of eternal life, and so it is with all who will call on the name of Jesus for salvation. No one has any more to offer to God for their redemption than this thief who died with Christ. We all must go to the Lord empty-handed, depending solely upon His grace to save us.

Two men died with Jesus that day. One went to be with Him in paradise, and one did not. One man was saved, and one was forever lost. How sad it is to see the unrepentant thief so close to the one who offered forgiveness die without trusting in Him.

Have *you* been born again? Do you the have the assurance of eternal life? Your salvation is not dependent on what church or denomination you belong to, being baptized, or being good enough to be acceptable to God. Receiving the gift of eternal life is based solely upon having a personal relationship with Jesus Christ and putting your trust for forgiveness in Him. Have you asked Jesus to be your Savior? It is important to understand that when a person asks Jesus to forgive them of their sins and to be their Savior, they are also accepting Him as Lord of their life. Jesus wants us to repent, meaning that He wants us to turn away from running our own lives and surrender ourselves to Him and His control. Understand that it is God who, over time, changes us, making us more like Christ. We cannot change ourselves.

When Jesus comes into your life, He does so, not only to forgive you of your sins but to radically transform you. It was after I accepted Jesus as my Savior that life became challenging for me spiritually. When you become a Christian, God will chisel away at the things in your life that He wants to change to make you more like His Son. God's chastening can be painful at times, but understand that if He doesn't chasten us, then we really don't belong to Him.

Perhaps you have prayed for God's forgiveness, but you still don't *feel* saved or *feel* forgiven. Feelings can be one of the greatest deceivers in your life. Past events that you've gone through, the rejection and hurt you've experienced—all have a tremendous effect on whether you feel saved and feel accepted by God, so *do not trust* your feelings. Trust God's promise that He will save you if you surrender your sins and your life to Him. Ask for His forgiveness and believe that He provides that forgiveness through the sacrificial death of His Son. Remember, the desire you have for salvation comes from God's calling you to come to Him, and Jesus said in John 6:37, "*him that cometh to me I will in no wise cast out.*" This means that He *will* accept you no matter what is in your past. He is calling you because He loves you, He wants to forgive you of all your sins, and He has *chosen you* to belong to Him.

You might argue, "But you don't know what I've done!" God knows all about your sin. He knows everything you've ever thought, said, and done; and He knows everything that you will ever think, say, and do in the future. Nothing is hidden from Almighty God. Matthew 12:31 tells us, "*All manner of sin and blasphemy shall be forgiven unto men.*" Jesus didn't say that *almost* all manner of sin and blasphemy shall be forgiven. He said *all* manner of sin and blasphemy shall be forgiven, so no matter how wicked your life has been and no matter what you've said or done, He will forgive you completely and forever. Psalms 103:12 says, "*As far as the east is from the west, so far hath he removed our transgressions from us.*" The distance between the east and the west is infinite. That is how far God separates you from your sins. Isaiah 1:18 tells us, "*Though your sins be as scarlet, they shall be as white as snow; though they be red like crimson, they shall be as wool.*" The precious blood of Jesus will make you *perfect* and *righteous* in God's eyes.

When is the best time to accept Christ? 2 Corinthians 6:2 tells us, "*Behold, now is the accepted time; behold, now is the day of salvation.*" If you have not invited Jesus into your life and asked Him to be your Lord and Savior, *now* is the time to trust Him; *today* is the day of salvation. He is waiting for you with open arms. Don't be like the impenitent thief that died without Christ. He was so close to the Savior, but tragically, he died without putting his trust in Him.

In prayer, confess to God that you are a sinner and that you need the forgiveness that only He can provide. Tell Him that you are willing to surrender your life to Him and allow Him to rule over you and make the decision to depend solely on the sacrificial death of the Lord Jesus for your forgiveness. Jesus is waiting to lovingly accept you right now.

If you have taken these steps to receive Christ, trust that He *has* forgiven you, not because of how things seem or how you feel. You can *know* that you are saved because of the promise of His Word. God does not lie, and He doesn't make mistakes. So trust Him.

Beginning with the book of John, read from the Bible each day. Also, find and attend a Bible-believing church that will help you grow in your faith. Finally, follow the Lord in baptism as a public confession of your decision to trust in Him.

Remember, there is not one sin that exists that the blood of Jesus Christ will not cover. No sin is unforgivable for the one who calls upon the name of the Lord for salvation, for whosoever does so *shall be saved!* Because of God's faithful promise, today can be the day of *your* salvation.

About the Author

———— ⌒ ————

Jon Hunter is a retired self-employed contractor from Central Ohio. Jon worked with his eldest son, Gabriel, and Sherry, his loving wife of forty-six years. His youngest son, Michael, lives in a nursing home in Orrville, Ohio. Jon became a born-again Christian when he was twenty years old. He believes that other than his salvation, his family is his greatest gift from God.